YOU
ARE A
BADASS
MINI BOOK

JEN SINCERO

T0364011

A Running Press® Miniature Edition™

Copyright © 2016 by Jen Sincero.

Adapted from *You Are a Badass: How to Stop Doubting Your Greatness and Start living an Awesome Life*, published in 2013 by Running Press.

Running Press
Hachette Book Group
1290 Avenue of the Americas, New York, NY 10104
www.runningpress.com
@Running_Press

First Edition: March 2016

Published by Running Press, an imprint of Perseus Books, LLC, a subsidiary of Hachette Book Group, Inc. The Running Press name and logo is a trademark of the Hachette Book Group.

The Hachette Speakers Bureau provides a wide range of authors for speaking events. To find out more, go to www.hachettespeakersbureau.com or call (866) 376-6591.

The publisher is not responsible for websites (or their content) that are not owned by the publisher.

ISBN: 978-0-7624-6008-3

Contents

INTRODUCTION

I'm assuming if you're reading this that there are some areas of your life that aren't looking so great. And that you know could be looking a whole lot better. This book is about getting mighty clear about what makes you happy and what makes you feel the most alive, and then creating it instead of pretending you can't have it. Or that you don't deserve it. Or that you're a greedy egomaniacal fathead for wanting more than you already have. It's about having the cojones to show up as the brightest, happiest, badassiest version of yourself, whatever that looks like to you.

HOW TO EMBRACE
YOUR INNER BADASS

LOVE THE ONE
YOU IS

Imagine what our world would be like if everyone loved themselves so much that they weren't threatened by other people's opinions or skin colors or sexual preferences or talents or education or possessions or lack of possessions or religious beliefs or customs or their general tendency to just be whoever the hell they are. Imagine how different your reality would be (and the reality of everyone surrounding you) if you woke up every morning certain of your own lovability and your critically important role on this planet. And if you poo pooed shame, guilt, self-doubt and self-loathing and allowed yourself to be, do and have everything your little heart desired.

That's the world I want to live in.

In the interest of perpetuating such radical, reality-altering self-love, here are some of the best ways to win yourself over again:

1. Appreciate How Special You Are

You are the only you that will ever be. You are kind of a big deal.

2. Drown Yourself in Affirmations

Trust me, I wouldn't do this to you unless I had to, but affirmations work. Find a few phrases that get to the heart of what you need to hear the most and repeat them all day long in your head, in the car, while you're walking down the street pretending to be on the phone, under your breath in line at the DMV. Write them on Post-it notes and stick them around your house, on your mirrors, in your refrigerator, in your car.

3. Ditch the Self-Deprecating Humor

Seemingly harmless jokes, over time, turn into seriously destructive beliefs. Our thoughts become our words, our words become our beliefs, our beliefs become our actions, our actions become our habits, and our habits become our realities. Just stop.

Also, notice the verbiage that runs through your mind when you're being the most heinous to yourself and come up with a new-and-improved response. For example, if every time you look in the mirror, your first thought is *yikes*, make a conscious effort to change it to *hi, gorgeous!*

4. **Let the Love In**

Receive compliments gracefully instead of countering with a disclaimer such as, "Oh, this ratty old thing?" Try this instead: "Thank-you." Period.

Take care of your body, too. Say nice things about your body, dress it up, and take it out. Move it, stretch it, nourish it, hydrate it, pay attention to it—the better our bodies feel, the happier and more productive we are.

5. Don't Compare Yourself to Others

Do not waste your precious time giving one single crap about what anybody else thinks of you. What other people think about you has nothing to do with you and everything to do with them.

The only questions you ever need to consider when making decisions about your life are 1) Is this something I want to be, do, or have? 2) Is this going to take me in the direction I want to go (not *should* go)? And 3) Is this going to screw over anybody else in the process? (Your mother being disappointed or your friends being outraged does not qualify as screwing someone over.)

All that matters is what's true for you, and if you can stay connected to that without straying, you will be a mighty superhero.

You are more than enough. Avoid comparison like the plague.

6. Forgive Yourself

You have screwed up in the past. You will screw up again. Dragging around guilt and self-criticism is beyond unhealthy and is utterly pointless, not to mention boring. Guilt, shame, and self-criticism are some of the most destructive forces in your life, which is why forgiving yourself is one of the most powerful. You aren't a better person for feeling guilty or bad about yourself, just a sadder one.

· 7. **Love Yourself**

Because it's the Holy Grail of happiness.

WHAT ARE YOU DOING HERE?

Every single person is born with unique and valuable gifts to share with the world. Once we figure out what ours are, and decide to live our lives putting them to use, that's when, and only when, the real party begins. Living a life on purpose is available to *everyone*. So if you're struggling or settling or completely confused about what you're supposed to do with your life, know that the answer is already here. It exists and so does the life you can't wait to create. You just need to get some clarity first.

Here are some guidelines on getting clear on who you are and what your calling is:

1. Be the Alien

Imagine that you're an alien floating around in outer space and you suddenly swoop down to earth and inhabit your own body. What is this person who you've inhabited so obviously awesome at? What do they have the most fun doing? What connections do they have? What resources and opportunities are available to them? How are you going to use this new body and this existence to create something fabulous and awesome starting right now?

This exercise is hugely helpful for getting a new perspective and stepping outside our boring-ass ruts of tired old excuses and lame habits. It can also be very useful in making you aware of all the staggering possibilities and resources that you have at your fingertips and take for granted or do not see.

2. Take the First Right Step

Instead of wasting hours and days and years trying to figure out your perfect next move, just DO something already. Oh the time we waste rolling ideas around in our heads, imagining what-ifs, coming up with perfect reasons why and then perfect reasons why not, tearing at our cuticles, making our friends and family carefully screen their calls in case it's us again, wanting to go over some ideas. Get out of your head and take action. You don't have to know exactly where it's going to take you, you just need to start with one thing that feels right and keep following right-feeling things and see where they lead.

3. Do Your Best Wherever You're At

Once you take this first step, it's possible that you won't land in your dream situation right away. You might land on a stepping-stone. Having a good attitude and being grateful for all the things that are helping you live the life of your dreams will not only make your life a more pleasant place to be, but it will also raise your frequency and attract the people and opportunities to you that will take you in the direction you want to go. Remember that you are going for it, you are bravely moving towards your dream, you are surrounded by unthinkable miracles and opportunities.

4. Don't Reinvent The Wheel

What things are people doing that you would love to do too? Who do you think is the coolest person ever? You don't need to invent your ideal life from scratch, you just need to figure out what makes you feel alive.

Get specific about the things in their lives that turn you on. Is it because they get to travel the world? Is it that they have a solid routine? Is it that they have no routine? Is it that they work alone? That they work in the nude? That they get to be outside all day? That they work with their hands? Their eyes? Their ears? Their animals? Their spouse? The more specific you get, the easier it will be to create a picture of what you want.

5. **Don't Get Caught Up in the Thunderbolt Hype**

I think one of the most paralyzing misconceptions is that we're all supposed to have one true calling that comes to us in a mighty flash of soul-defining insight. Let yourself off the hook if you don't have that one, big, perfect thing that you know you came here to do, and feel good about the fact that you'll probably fulfill several callings throughout your life. Follow what feels good in the moment, every moment, and it will lead you through a most excellent life.

6. **Follow Your Fantasies**

What do you fantasize about when you're staring out the window of a train, or before you go to sleep at night, or when you're pretending to listen to someone really boring talk your ear off? Tap into what brings you great joy instead of what you think you need to do to survive. Our fantasies are the most revealing peepholes into who we are and what we think is awesome. They are our realities in an excuse-free world. What if you decided to do the most outrageous, most exciting thing you ever dared fantasize about, regardless of what anyone, including your terrified self, thought?

THAT would be living.

7. Love yourself

Like you're the only you there is.

HOW TO TAP INTO THE MOTHER LODE

THE G WORD

Wherever you happen to stand on the God issue, let me just say that that this whole improving your life thing is going to be a lot easier if you have an open mind about it. Call it whatever you want—God, Goddess, The Big Guy, The Universe, Source Energy, Higher Power, The Grand Poobah, gut, intuition, Spirit,

The Force, The Zone, The Lord, The Vortex, The Mother Lode—it doesn't matter. Whatever you choose to call it isn't important, what is important is that you start to develop an awareness of, and a relationship with, the Source Energy that's surrounding you and within you (which is all the same energy), and which will be your best pal ever if you give it a chance. Because here's the thing: All of us are connected to this limitless power and most of us aren't using but a fraction of it.

When you learn to consciously master the energetic realm, believe in the not yet seen, and stay in your highest frequency, you harness your innate power to create the reality you desire.

MEDITATION 101

Meditation, otherwise known as sitting still and thinking about nothing, is one of those things that can be just as stupidly simple as it is surprisingly hard.

That's all I have to do to connect with Source Energy? Sit there and do nothing? It can't be that easy.

Well . . . it is. And it's not.

Which is why it's called a meditation *practice.*

When you shut up and meditate for even five minutes and start to really notice the thoughts that are squirreling around in your brain, it's rather . . . illuminating. The goal is to quiet your mind of the chatter so you can connect to Source Energy and instead listen to your inner guidance. Aside from being one of the most powerful tools in our consciousness-raising toolbox, meditation is a much-needed respite from the madness, and will help us from becoming a bunch of scatterbrained ding-dongs as we zoom around our brave, and extremely exciting, digitized new world.

There's no right way or wrong way

to do this, no set amount of time (try starting with five or ten minutes and working your way up), no correct things to feel, no rules about how you have to sit or where you have to do it. All that matters is that you do it if you want to massively improve your life. Because when we meditate, we practice getting into The Vortex and connecting to Source Energy, which automatically brings us into the present moment, relieves stress, opens us up to receive unlimited information and ideas, puts us in a good mood, and helps us love ourselves.

Here are the extremely short and simple steps of some different ways to meditate:

Basic Meditation

- Sit in a comfortable, cross-legged position on the floor, or in a chair, with your hands on your knees or in your lap. Sit up straight and relax your entire face, especially your jaw and your forehead.
- Close your eyes, or, if it helps you focus and not fall asleep, keep them open and gaze softly at a spot on the ground a couple feet

in front of you. Or, try lighting a candle, placing it on the floor in front of you, and focusing on that.

- Notice your breath moving in and out of your body. You don't have to breathe in any special way. Just focus on it.
- Gently release any thoughts that come into your brain and re-focus on your breathing. Keep your mind as clear and empty as possible and listen for intuitive hits that may or may not come through.
- Experiment with mantras. Sometimes when the squirrels in

my head are particularly active, I bring in a mantra to chase them out. I repeat a word or phrase in my mind like "love" or "thank you" or "yes, please" or "om"— something that makes me feel good and is fairly neutral, but you could use a mantra like "meatloaf" I guess if that's your thing.

Tah-dah! That's it.

YOUR BRAIN
IS YOUR BITCH

Remember, everything you desire already exists. You just have to shift your perception in order to see it made manifest. Your job isn't to know the *how*, it's to know the *what* and to be open to discovering, and receiving, the *how*.

Keep your thoughts directed at your goal, do everything that you DO know how to do to make it happen, decide with unwavering determination that it will happen, and be on the lookout for the opportunity.

The moment you have the audacity to start believing in the not-yet seen, your reality will begin to shift.

Here are some tried-and-true ways to show your brain who's driving the bus:

1. Ask and it is Given

Get quiet, get in The Zone, and get in touch with Source Energy. Clear out the chatter in your brain and create a clean, uncluttered space to impress the thoughts of what you want into the giant thinking substance that is Source Energy. Ask for what you want, send out a nice, clear message in a nice, clear space and begin the manifestation process.

2. Act As If

If you want something badly, even if you don't have any evidence that it's possible for you to attain, act as if it is. Fake it until you make it. Do it in spite of yourself.

3. Make a Vision Board

Cut out pictures of places, people, things, and experiences that you want in your life, paste them onto a board and hang it somewhere where you'll see it all day long. I've seen people have completely insane results with this. They've manifested, down to the tiniest details, the exact home or piece of furniture or place of employment that they put on their board. It's freaky- deaky. And super easy. Give it a shot.

4. Surround Yourself with People Who Think the Way You Want to Think

Surround yourself with people who act on their big ideas, who take action on making positive change in the world and who see nothing as out of their reach. Being around inspired, visionary, enthusiastic people who are living their truths is one of the fastest ways to massively transform your life.

5. Love Yourself

Unless you have a better idea.

GIVE AND LET GIVE

We live in a universe of give and receive, breathe and exhale, live and die, suck and awesome. Each side depends on the other, and each is relative to the other— every action has an equal and opposite reaction—so the more you give, the more you receive. And vice versa.

If you want to attract good things and feelings into your life, send awesomeness out to everyone around you. Here are some good ways to get in the give-and-take flow, yo:

- If you haven't already, pick one or two causes that have real meaning to you and give to them every month. Give however much time or money you can, but do it consistently so it becomes a habit and becomes part of who you are.
- Leave a dollar more than you normally would every time you tip. Or ten.
- If someone is being snarky, instead of sinking to their level and being snarky back, raise them up by giving them the love.
- Smile, compliment, and crack

people up as often as possible.

- Stop and feel in your body how great it feels when you give and receive, raise your frequency and expect more good things to come your way.
- **Love yourself**, and everybody benefits.

FORGIVE OR FESTER

Lugging around guilt, shame, resentment and self-loathing is your less-than-badass-self running the show, pitching a fit, demanding to be right and to be seen. Your higher self, on the other hand, could give a crap about what anybody else thinks or does because your higher self is madly in love with you and that's all that matters. Whatever happened, happened. Holding on will not change this fact, it will just keep the negative feelings from the past alive, keep you a prisoner to your pain and lower your frequency.

The moment you decide to forgive and let your negative feelings melt away, you are on the road to freedom.

Now how do you actually let it all go? How do you forgive the stupid bastard?

1. Find Compassion

Finding compassion for yourself or someone else who did something so so so so awful is like pulling a bullet out of your arm: You may kick and scream and hate it at first, but, in the long run, it's the only way to start the real healing.

One of the best tricks for doing this is to imagine the person you're resentful of as a little kid who is acting out of fear, doing the best they can to protect themselves and attempting to deal with their own suffering in the only way they know how.

2. Decide You'd Rather Be Happy Than Right

Yes, your idiot friend should have paid the parking ticket she got when she borrowed your car, but if she doesn't see it that way, instead of spinning out on it for days, wouldn't it feel so much better to just let it go? Is it really worth lugging around all those foul feelings just so you can be right? Think to yourself, "what do I have to do or not do, or think or not think, right now, to be happy?" And if the answer is "let the jackass think she's right" then so be it.

3. Look at It from All Angles

It's important to remember that everyone is living in their own self-created illusion, and that you have no idea what they're acting out or where they're coming from.

Look at it from another perspective, loosen your stranglehold on it being *my way or the highway*, let some air in, and you may be surprised how quickly resentment flies out the window.

4. **Fuggetaboutit**

Once you've truly forgiven someone, wipe the slate clean. So often we form judgments about people and then, no matter what they do, we see them through the lens of that judgment. Which means we're just waiting for them to piss us off again. What you focus on, you create more of, and if you keep expecting people to annoy you they will do just that. Focus on their finer points and encourage their good behavior if you want to create more of it.

5. Love Yourself

You deserve it.

HOW TO GET OVER YOUR BS ALREADY

PROCRASTINATION AND PERFECTION

Procrastination is one of the most popular forms of self-sabotage because it's really easy.

There are so many fun things you can do in order to procrastinate, and there's no lack of other people who are totally psyched to procrastinate with you.

And while it can be super fun in the moment, eventually the naughtiness buzz wears off and you're sitting there a few years later, feeling like a loser, wondering why the hell you still haven't gotten your act together. And why other people you know are getting big fat promotions at their jobs or taking trips around the world or talking about the latest orphanage they've opened in Cambodia on NPR.

If you're serious about changing your life, you'll find a way. If you're not, you'll find an excuse.

In the interest of getting you where

you want to go in this lifetime, here are some tried-and-true tips to help you stop procrastinating:

1. Remember That Done is Better Than Perfect

Just get the damn website up already or send out the mailer or make the sales calls or book the gig even though you're not totally ready yet. Nobody else cares or will probably even notice that everything isn't one hundred percent perfect—and, quite honestly, nothing ever will be one hundred percent perfect anyway so you might as well start now. There's no better way to get things done than to already be rolling along—momentum is a wonderful thing, not to mention highly underrated, so get off your ass and get started. NOW!

2. Notice Where You Stop

When you're working on whatever you're working on (or whatever you're pretending to work on) where exactly do you stop? Is it when you have to do the research? Make the scary phone calls? Figure out how to raise the money? Right after you start? When you have to commit? When it starts getting good? Right before it takes off? Before you even get out of bed?

If you can pinpoint the precise moment that you say, "Screw it—I'm outta here!" you can prepare yourself for hitting the oil slick by hiring coaches or assistants or psyching yourself up or delegating that particular part of it out, or removing known distractions.

Once you become aware of what your weak spots are, you can start to protect yourself against them. Turn off the Internet and phone while you're working. Make the kitchen off-limits until you're done if you constantly find yourself standing in front of the open refrigerator door in a stupor.

3. Make a Bet on Your Success

A good way to make yourself accountable is to make a bet with someone who will hold you to it. Tell them that if you don't meet your deadline, you'll donate one thousand dollars (or some amount that feels painful to lose, but realistic) to a group or cause that makes your flesh crawl. You might find this kind of horror works wonders for your self-discipline.

4. **Own It and Work with It**

If you're the kind of person who blows everything off until the last minute, and you know this about yourself, why waste your time freaking out while you're not doing what you're supposed to be doing? Go to the damn beach, have a cocktail, and when the pressure's on, get down to business. There's nothing worse than time wasted pretending to work or stressing out while trying to have fun—no work gets done and no fun is had. It's the worst of both worlds. Figure out how much time you truly need to get the job done, and go do something else until the clock starts ticking.

5. Love Yourself

Right now, wherever you're at.

MILLIONS OF MIRRORS

We're all attracted to, as well as turned off by, various things about other people. And the things that stand out the most to us are the things that remind us the most of ourselves. This is because other people are like mirrors for us: If somebody bugs you, you're projecting onto them something that you don't like about yourself, and if you think they're awesome, they're reflecting back something that you see in yourself that you like (even if it's not developed in you yet). I know this sounds like I'm making a massive generalization, but just stay with me here.

The things that bother us about other people bother us because they remind us of something that we don't like about ourselves. Or their behavior triggers a fear or insecurity that we have, but may not realize we have.

None of us care to admit that we're dishonest, conceited, insecure, bullies, unethical, mean, bossy, stupid, lazy, etc., but that's what attracted you to the people you notice it in, and them to you, in the first place.

Same thing goes with what people throw at us. Would you be offended if someone kept making fun of how short you were if you were six feet tall? It most likely wouldn't even register, or if it did, you'd just think they were kind of strange. But if they teased you about being bossy, and deep down you feared you were, it would definitely get your attention.

What you focus on you create more of in your life. If you're consciously or subconsciously focused on certain beliefs about who you are, or who you want to be or who you do not want to be, you will attract people who mirror those traits right back at you.

So how can you get rid of your lame-o projections and judgments and grace the world with your highest, most unapologetic self?

1. Own Your Ugly

Start noticing the things that drive you nuts about other people, and, instead of complaining or judging or getting defensive about them, use them as a mirror. Get mighty real with yourself – is this quality something you have yourself? Or does it remind you of something you're actively trying to suppress? Or that you're actively doing just the opposite of? Or that you're threatened by? Become fascinated by, instead of furious about, the irritants surrounding you and get yer learnin on.

2. Question Your Ugly

Once you discover what part of yourself you're projecting onto the person who is presently bugging the living crap out of you, you can start letting it go. Begin by asking yourself:

- Who do I need to be for this situation not to bother me?
- What am I getting out of being this way?
- How would I feel if I wasn't this way?

3. **Love Yourself**

Fiercely, loyally, unapologetically.

HOW TO KICK SOME ASS

THE ALMIGHTY DECISION

When you make a no-nonsense decision, you sign up fully and keep moving towards your goal, regardless of what's flung in your path. And stuff will most definitely get flung, which is why making the decision is so crucial—this shit is not for sissies. The moment it gets hard or expensive or puts you at risk of looking like a moron, if you haven't made the decision, you'll quit. If it wasn't uncomfortable, everyone would be out there all in love with their fabulous lives.

So often, we pretend we've made a decision, when what we've really done is signed up to try until it gets too uncomfortable.

This is where being connected to your desire and Source Energy, and having an unshakable belief in the not-yet seen, is so critical. There are plenty of times when we get a brilliant idea and it temporarily fails or it pushes us into unfamiliar territory. If we don't have a strong connection to the truth, a blazing desire, and an unflinching belief in our own vision before it's manifested, we'll fall prey to our own fears and everyone else's fears that it's not possible and give up, instead of course-correcting or pushing on through and bringing it to life.

There are plenty of people out there in the world living the kind of life you only dream about living, many of whom are far less fabulous and talented than you are. They key to their success is that they decided to go for it, they stopped listening to their tired old excuses, changed their lousy habits, and got the fuck on the fuck.

Here's how you can, too:

1. Want It Bad

If you're going to push through major obstacles to reach your goal, you can't just want to want to; you need to be in a full-on tizzy of excitement about what it is you're going after and hold onto it like a pit bull. In order to do this you need to have the audacity to be honest about what you really want to do, not what you *should* do, believe it's available to you regardless of any evidence otherwise, and go for it.

2. Eliminate the Negotiation Process

The old you, the one who has not yet decided to kick ass, is in the past. Stay present and do not, even for a second, look backwards or entertain any ideas of straying from your decision. Think only of the new you. Decisions are not up for negotiation.

3. Stick Like Glue

In order to change your life and start living a new one that you've never lived before, your faith in miracles—and yourself—must be greater than your fear. However easy or rough the process is, you have to be willing to fall down, get up, look stupid, cry, laugh, make a mess, clean it up and not stop until you get there. No matter what.

4. Love Yourself

You can do anything.

MONEY, YOUR NEW BEST FRIEND

Here's the thing: Making money isn't only about the money, just as losing weight isn't only about losing weight and finding your soul mate isn't only about finding your soul mate. It's about who you become and what you believe is possible for yourself.

We live in a Universe that is vibrating with energy. Our Universe is abundant, and everything you desire is here, in this moment, waiting for you to shift your perception and your energy and receive it. Money included.

Money is energy like anything else, and when you're operating at a high frequency with no resistance to it, and take right action, you can manifest the money you desire. We all know that we have to work to make money, we've been taught that all our lives, but what we're not taught is that we must also align our energy with the financial abundance we seek. If you are going to play a bigger game—i.e. quit your ho-hum job and invest in your own business, buy a house, send your kids to private schools, hire a coach, hire a housecleaner, buy a new mattress, etc.—you are going to need money. And it will either be the money you have, or you are going to need to manifest the money if you don't have it already. And manifesting it is going to be pretty damn hard if you insist that not only is it not there for you, but that you aren't the kind of person who could ever make it or pay it off if you borrowed it.

In order to transform your life, you may have to spend the money you do have, get a loan, sell something, borrow from a friend, put it on your credit card or manifest it in some other way. Which is going to go against some pretty deep-seated beliefs we've all been raised with about how going into debt is irresponsible. This is about taking a leap of faith into a new realm that you strongly desire to be in, demanding of yourself that you rise to the occasion and start living your damn life already.

Our relationship with money is just as important as the action we take to manifest it, which is one reason why so many people who work their asses off their whole lives but have lousy energy around money are left wondering why they have nothing to show for it.

First Rule of Wealth Consciousness: Come from a Place of Abundance, Not Lack

When we say we want money for something, we often come from a place of "I don't have it, it does not exist, so I need to create it." This has us focusing on, and believing in, lack, thereby lowering our frequency and attracting more lack.

When we say, "I am manifesting five

grand to go on a trip to Italy you just watch me," our faith in the yet unseen is strong and our frequency is high. Thus, so is our ability to attract money. Believe that you can have what you desire, that it really truly already exists, and then go out and get it.

Second Rule of Wealth Consciousness: Get Clear on Where You're At

Start healing your relationship with money. Sit your broke ass down and write a letter to money and then break it down, sentence by sentence, and create some new money affirmations. Repeat your new affirmations and feel them in your bones. Replace your story that "I resent needing money" with "I'm grateful to money for helping me live such an awesome life."

Third Rule of Wealth Consciousness: Get Clear on Where You Desire to Be

We all need money. We need it to feed ourselves, buy clothes, get shelter, water, medicine, etc. Once it goes beyond basic survival, however, and we get into the arena of how much money we "need," if we've got guilt and judgment and terror over what it means to have it and what people will think of us if we do, this is where all hell is gonna break loose.

Feeling like you don't deserve the things that make you the happiest and best version of yourself, because it's greedy or is asking too much, ultimately rips off the rest of the world because you aren't being fully supported and, as a result, aren't sharing your highest frequency with the world.

Be your best, do your best, demand

the best, expect the best, receive the best, and put your best out into the world so everyone can receive your best, too.

Fourth Rule of Wealth Consciousness: Raise Your Frequency

Nothing has any value other than the value we put on it. If we believe we are worth ten dollars an hour, that's the frequency we'll put out and that's the kind of client or job we'll attract. If we believe we're worth one thousand dollars an hour, that's the frequency we'll put out and that's the kind of client or employment opportunities we'll attract.

In order to create wealth, you must bring yourself into energetic alignment with the money you desire to manifest. If you're nowhere near whe re you want to be, keep pushing yourself to raise your prices or seek higher paying jobs. Surround yourself with higher frequency experiences and people. Beef up your education and know-how. Make vision boards of what you want your life to look like. Again, raising your frequency is like developing a muscle – strengthening it is a process.

Fifth Rule of Wealth Consciousness: Get Real

There is a big difference between walking around saying you want to make a million dollars a year, and having crystal clear intentions, fierce desire and hell-bent action towards specific goals.

Start by thinking about the life you'd love to live and why, figure out exactly how much money you need to manifest to make it happen. How much money do you now need to make per year? Per month? Per hour? The Universe responds to details. The Universe responds to energy. The Universe responds to badasses.

Lame, vague goals are the best way to live a lame, vague life. Decide what it is you want and write down the exact cost.

Then, make it urgent. The money is there if you really, truly desire it. The trick is to treat your dreams with this same urgency and determination as, say, paying rent or having a rotten tooth pulled.

Sixth Rule of Wealth Consciousness: Get Hungry

Do every single thing you can think of to manifest this money/new lifestyle, whether you've got your own business or you work for someone else. Listen to everyone around you speak with new ears – is there an opportunity for a new, better paying situation there that you may have not noticed before? Is there a position you can create or suggest that would get you at your desired income level? It's not your job to know the *how*, it's your job to ask for what you want and wait to discover the *how*, then take action. Continue to do everything humanly possible to magnetize it to you, and then surrender to The Universe and be on the lookout for something unexpected to come in.

Seventh Rule of Wealth Consciousness: Love Yourself

And you will have it all.

BEAM ME UP, SCOTTY

Whatever you desire to do with your precious life—write jokes or rock out or start a business or learn to speak Greek or quit your job or raise a bunch of kids or fall in love or lose your flab or open orphanages around the world or direct movies or save dolphins or make millions—believe that it's possible. And that it's available to you. And that you deserve to be/do/have it.

Why not?

Give yourself the permission and the means (yes, this includes the money), to be who you are REGARDLESS OF WHAT ANYBODY ELSE THINKS OR BELIEVES IS POSSIBLE. Do not deny yourself the life you want to live because you're worried you're not good enough or that you'll be judged or that it's too risky, because who does that benefit? No one, that's who. When you live your life doing the things that turn you on, that you're good at, that bring you joy, that make you shove stuff in people's faces and scream, "check this out!!!" you walk around so lit up that you shoot sunbeams out of yer eyeballs. Which automatically lights up the world around you. Which is precisely why you are here: To shine your big ass ball of fire onto this world of ours. A world that literally depends upon light to survive.

You are powerful. You are loved. You are surrounded by miracles.

Believe, *really* believe that what you desire is here and available to you. And you can have it all.

Love Yourself

You are a badass.

For a complete course in changing your life, fork over the $16.00 for a copy of Jen Sincero's *You Are a Badass: How to Stop Doubting Your Greatness and Start Living an Awesome Life.*

This book has been bound using handcraft methods and Smyth-sewn to ensure durability.

The text was written by Jen Sincero.

The text was abridged and edited by Jessica Fromm.

Designed by Joshua McDonnell.

The text was set in Avenir, Brandon, & Garamound